How to Motivate Yourself and Others

How to Motivate Yourself and Others

A Christians Approach to Motivation

From the Success in Christian Living series—a practical approach to achieving your goals for time, money, motivation, and human potential.

by Dennis E. Hensley

Published by Warner Press
Anderson, Indiana

All Scripture passages, unless otherwise indicated, are from the Holy Bible, King James Version ©1972 *by Thomas Nelson, Revised Standard Version* ©1972, *by Thomas Nelson, or New International Version* ©1987 *by New York International Bible Society.*

Warner Press, Inc.
Arlo F. Newell, Editor in Chief
Dan Harman, Book Editor
Caroline Smith, Editor

Contents

Page

Introduction:

An Excitement for Life

A man once went to see his physician. After a complete examination the man asked, "What's wrong with me, Doc?" The physician replied, "Nothing. You're just lazy." The man nodded agreement and said, "Well, then, tell me the medical term for it so I can tell my wife."

Perhaps you've known a few people like that. Rather than be motivated to get more accomplished, they prefer to develop an excuse for their continued lack of productivity. Trying to build a fire under these people seems an effort in futility, for the only one who gets hot is you—and all under the collar.

Still, we all need the help of others. Whether you are the chairperson of a large corporation or the chairperson of a church board, you need people who will be motivated to carry out your plans. Whether you are the First Lady of a nation or the First Lady of a family, you need to know how to organize, inspire, and direct those persons you are overseeing.

That is the purpose of this book. We are going to learn the many ways that the Bible has taught us how to be energetic and goal-oriented Christians and how we can transfer our God-honoring enthusiasm to others.

Some people may find it difficult to focus upon a single attribute of their lives that succinctly and tightly and coherently summarizes what it is they believe in—that is to say, what it is that is their credo.

I am not such a person. I can tell you my attitudes toward busi-

ness, study, and advancement in one word. I can explain my optimistic outlook for my future and my current self-fulfillment at
what I'm involved in, in one word. That word is EXCITEMENT.

I believe in excitement. And I'm not talking about the Saturday
afternoon Tarzan matinee excitement of children. No, what I
mean is the deep-down, self-generated, self-motivated, self-sus-
tained kind of excitement that comes when you challenge yourself
with wondrous goals and you strive to reach your full potential.

I'm talking about the excitement that comes when you know
that you know who you are and what you can do—and you're
overjoyed about it. It's the kind of excitement that makes you
believe that not only can you do something, but that you will do
something—and that you can hardly wait to get started.

Factory owners and employers of large numbers of people have
long realized that when a person likes her or his job and is excited
about what she or he does, the work output of that person is
much greater than average. For this reason, employers spend vast
sums of cash on creating pleasing office decors, making pleasant
lunchroom facilities, on improving heating, lighting, ventilation,
furniture, and equipment, just so that employees will be glad to
come to work—so that they will be excited about what they're
doing.

But, my own belief is that each man and woman should be self-
excited. Yes, that's right: self-excited. We should say, "I'm excited
about what I do! I've got goals and challenges, vistas, priorities,
missions, and objectives, and my whole life is an exciting adven-
ture. I'm so excited about who I am and what I have facing me,
that there is no way I can fail. This is all too much fun."

When you begin to see responsibility as "quest," you'll be ready
for more of it. When you begin to see your day-to-day employ-
ment as a series of important missions, then you will become
organized. When you begin to think of obstacles as opportunities,
of setbacks as experiences, and of pressures as signs of your ability
to function under duress, then you will be able to maintain your
excitement about life. And when you maintain your excitement,
you will succeed.

Complaining needs to be replaced with excitement. I know that
we all have what seem to be monumental heartbreaking stresses.

Some of you are thinking, What? Excited? How can I be excited when I just got turned down for a raise? Or What? Excited when I just learned that my house needs a new roof? Who's going to get excited about that?

You should.

With the right amount of excitement you can turn a bad situation into a golden opportunity.

In 1971 I was a private first class in the army. On January 2, my mother's birthday, I was transferred to South Vietnam and told that for the next year I would be working as a counselor inside of a military prison. Now, how hard do you want to make it on someone: I was eleven thousand miles from home; I was in a foreign country; I was in the middle of a war zone; and for twelve hours a day I was locked inside a prison.

I had two options open to me: I could be like many of the other men who moped, counted days, groaned about homesickness, and generally shifted their beings into neutral for a full year of their lives. Or I could get excited. I chose the latter: I got excited.

I approached the prison commandant and the chaplain on the idea of forming a prison choir, and within six weeks we had thirty-five prisoners who were not only attending chapel service, but who were also singing in the choir. Next, I told my officers that if they would buy some cheap guitars in Saigon, I would start giving them music lessons. Soon, nine lieutenants, captains, and majors were spending their free time "pickin' and grinnin.'"

Next, I got some buddies together and we convinced the supply sergeant to give us some lumber, old tarpaulins, some screens, and extra bricks, and we spent two months of evenings building ourselves a coffeehouse where we could sit and talk or write letters or listen to the radio. I later helped put together a base extension library inside of the prison, and also began to hold rap sessions in the chapel for the prisoners.

Time moved along quickly for me. And along the way, I was promoted to sergeant, awarded five letters of commendation, two unit citations, and six medals.

When you're excited—when you make yourself become excited about your situation, no matter how dreadful it may seem—you will be astounded by the results.

When people infuse excitement into their lives, they give themselves perspective. Perspective is balance. With the right perspective of things, you're able to see that you are never presented more challenge than you are given spirit to face. With the right perspective you are able to see that God never hands you more setbacks than he gives you opportunities to go forward. Life has balance when you offset the weight of disappointments with the buoyancy of excitement.

Excitement also infuses honesty and sincerity into your life. When you get up in the morning and look into the mirror and say, Today I am going to give people a dollar and a half of service for every dollar I am paid, you will never find yourself shortchanging anyone. Instead, people will say, How did we ever get along before she came? or Don't you wish we had another one like him?

No, friends, I have no difficulty whatsoever in telling you how it is that I can say, This I believe in. It's excitement. I'm excited that I have a God who watches over me, a wife and two children who love me, a job that challenges me, friends who enjoy my company, and a future that proves that life gets better and better each day. I like to think that I am like the Alcoa Company that claimed in its commercials, "We can't wait, we can't wait for tomorrow; Alcoa can't wait!" Well, I feel that same excitement; I can't wait, I can't wait for tomorrow. Today is so exciting, tomorrow can only be better.

Let me then share my philosophy with you. I suggest that you give your life a challenge, that you get yourself a natural perspective and balance, that you get yourself a sense of coherency, that you get yourself a positive attitude about life.

In short, that you get yourself EXCITED.

If you feel the urge to rise to your maximum potential abilities and to help others on your way up, turn now to the following chapters and learn the timeless lessons of leadership. You are fearfully and wonderfully made. Now is the time to discover the amazing gifts that lie within you.

Part 1
Personal Dynamics

Chapter 1:

Four Important Words

Before a person can move a nation that person must first learn to move herself or himself. For that reason, we are first going to examine ways in which you can motivate yourself.

Personal motivation can vary greatly at different stages of our lives. Our desires, needs, wants, goals, and ambitions change as we age and mature. The sporty hot rod you wanted at age sixteen may not hold the same appeal for you at age forty-six the way a new Cadillac does. The prestigious high school diploma you earned at age eighteen may seem a modest achievement ten years later at your class reunion as you stand near classmates who are teachers, surgeons, or ministers.

For some people the reassessment of goals and needs can be traumatic. What should be seen as exciting new challenges can be wrongfully viewed as threatening ordeals. I know this. I've felt those anxieties myself, those days of wondering whether life was passing me by or those moments when I felt that everyone was getting ahead except me. But some of those bad times turned out to be the best learning experiences on how to cope and move on.

Mark Twain once wrote, "When I was eighteen, my father was the biggest fool I'd ever known. When I was twenty-one, I was amazed at how much the old fellow had learned in just three short years."

That's how life often is. We see changes occurring all around us but seldom realize that the most significant changes are taking place within us.

That's true of our growth as Christians, too. Today I can look back over four decades of living and realize, only now, that the seemingly overwhelming challenges or trials of previous years were really opportunities and experiences God was providing me for later use.

I'm now slower to react positively or negatively to life's circumstances. I wait for God's leading. I've grown and matured as a Christian; or, as I've confessed to friends, I've learned a lot since I knew it all.

My growth as a Christian can best be summarized in four words: priorities, confidence, perspective, and forgiveness.

Priorities

The priorities of our Christian walk should begin with service to God. I learned to make God the first priority in my life after he proved to me that I was his first priority.

In 1978 my wife had complications during labor with our second child. Then the doctors told us our child would be stillborn. We were emotionally crushed. We hugged each other and cried for hours. We were terribly distraught over the death of our baby.

Nine hours later my wife was taken into the delivery room. Miraculously, a faint heartbeat was discovered in our daughter. She was rushed to a special intensive care unit at a children's hospital where, for days, she was treated around the clock.

But she lived. Today she is a healthy and happy child. Each time my wife and I recall how close we came to losing Jeanette, our hearts fill with incredible joy over the realization that she's here with us. How we love her!

With that in mind, I often sit in awe when I equate that to the sacrifice God the Father made of his Son, Jesus. How could God yield his dearest love for the likes of a sinner like me?

The only answer is that my salvation was the most important of God's priorities. Can I, then, make God any less than my top priority? No, I dare not.

Confidence

My confidence as a Christian has increased in measured amounts over the years. As a teen-ager, I was embarrassed even to stand in front of a group to share my testimony. Today I teach Sunday school to a large class of adults each week and I lecture to hundreds of people nationwide at various conferences and conventions.

How did I gain this confidence? I spent nine years working toward earning a doctoral degree in literature and linguistics. When the day came to defend my doctoral dissertation before a panel of five professors, I was ready and eager. I had prepared myself diligently and, as a result, I sailed through the defense without a hitch.

It occurred to me then, as never before, that confidence as a Christian also comes from preparation. The more grounded in the Word I became, the more able I would be to teach it, share it, and proclaim it.

This led me to focus more time on prayer and Bible study. Shortly thereafter I was offered opportunities to teach other Christians. Preparation led to confidence, and confidence led to opportunity.

Perspective

My perspective on my life as a Christian was gained during a twelve-month stint in South Vietnam as a sergeant in the army. I worked as a chaplain's aide and bodyguard. The work was hard, the weather terrible, and the assignments often life-threatening.

Through it all, however, I realized that my security in Christ gave me a comfort that many other soldiers did not have. I didn't relish the idea of being in a war zone, but I knew that God was with me and that God would use the experience to make me a better person.

In later years I faced certain hardships and setbacks—a lost job, an automobile accident, a facial paralysis, a bankrupt stock investment—but I was able to shrug each one off. I lived through a war, I'd remind myself, so what's this compared to that? With that kind of perspective, I found I could handle anything life could throw at me.

Forgiveness

And finally, the development of forgiveness in my life helped me understand my continuous relationship with God. Prior to becoming a parent, I sometimes felt that the Bible was too nonchalant about forgiving sins. It taught that by confessing, repenting, and praying, we could receive forgiveness from God.

As a business person, that baffled me. Shouldn't there be more to the deal, I wondered? Shouldn't I have to offer some sort of trade-off or barter agreement? After all, I came often before God asking forgiveness of my sins. Surely, God's patience would eventually run short and he would want something more tangible, right?

Actually, no. Just asking for forgiveness was enough.

Today, when my son or daughter makes a mistake or disobeys me or falls short of my expectations, and then he or she apologizes, I never fail to say, "That's all right. I can see that you're really sorry."

My love for my children is boundless in its patience and forgiveness. How much more must God's patience and forgiveness be with and for me.

With growth, I learn more each day about God. I'm more spiritually mature today than I was at seventeen, but not nearly as mature in the Lord as I'll be at fifty-seven. I never intend to stop growing in God's grace.

Part of the process of growing in grace calls for us to keep spiritually attuned to God. All respected leaders have understood the value of spiritual strength, and you should, too.

Chapter 2:

The Power of Spirit

D uring the Vietnam War I served as a chaplain's assistant at Long Binh, South Vietnam. Every Sunday morning the commanding general of our brigade would arrive at our chapel, his spit-shined and starched combat uniform all in order, and he would actively participate in our services.

This unswerving habit impressed me so much that one morning I found the courage to ask the general about it.

"I'm delighted to see you in our services on Sundays, sir," I said, "but I'm amazed that you can find the time. You're in charge of every M.P. here in Vietnam, you're contending with a war, and your schedule of meetings and inspections is second to no one's. I don't see how you can be here every week."

The general fixed his clear gray eyes on me. "I have to," he asserted. "My spirit requires it."

I wrinkled my forehead.

"A man's spirit is his source of extra strength," the general explained. "It gets him back on his feet after the third knockdown; it makes him push ahead when the cause seems hopeless; it gives him a shield of faith which protects him. Give me a man with an intact spirit and I'll give you a man who can't be defeated. I, myself, want to be that kind of unbreakable, undefeatable man. So, every Sunday I replenish my spirit with an hour of meditation and worship."

Until then I don't think I had really considered spiritual replenishment as having a direct bearing upon my secular life. But the general's words caused me to reconsider that.

When I started to catalog the ways we Americans use references to spirit, I discovered that there were as many secular applications to the word as there were religious ones. Both, however, had the same basic underlying definitions and all were positive forces.

One use of spirit refers to liveliness and enthusiasm, as in "a spirited horse" or "spirited competition." Another refers to a feeling of unified strength for a noble cause as in the spirit of "76" or "*esprit de corps.*" Yet another refers to fair and honest judgment, as in the application of "the spirit of the law" over the letter of the law.

So it is, then, that the very word *spirit* connotes power, purpose, and goodness. What three better qualities could a Christian desire?

But how ironic it is that we seldom really tap this mysterious source of strength. We are more than ready to read and study and attend classes to discipline our minds, and we will jog and swim and diet to strengthen our bodies, but when it comes to spirit building we do very little.

We should occasionally make time to take a long, quiet walk in the woods. We should frequent our places of worship. We should visit a trusted friend and verbally share some of our dreams and anxieties and feelings and emotions with him or her. We should do something now and then for the benefit of humankind—something more than pitching a quarter into a charity canister—something motivated by altruistic love rather than profit.

Several years ago, I had a friend named Chuck who was an insurance agent. Chuck was active in the church I attended. I used to watch that guy closely. He attended four services a week, served as a leader and Sunday school teacher, and had many, many friends in that church. But Chuck never talked about insurance there. Church was where Chuck refreshed his spirit. It was where he recharged his secret source of extra power.

As I watched Chuck, judged the way he served the church, and observed the way he seemed to be competent and contented, I learned to trust this strongly spirited man. One day I phoned him for advice regarding life insurance coverage for my family, and I eventually bought policies from him for my wife and son. I later learned that several other people in the church also had purchased policies from Chuck. He had the right spirit, and we all wanted him in our corner.

More recently, I have been reading about and talking with some of the greatest insurance salespeople in our country. I am intrigued by the emphasis these men and women put on spiritual strength.

For example, in *The Sullivan Method* (R & R Newkirk), an outstanding book on how to sell deferred compensation plans, Frank E. Sullivan offers his readers a chart that shows how one of his working weeks runs. Six out of seven days begin by attending church: and that example comes from a man who has earned his CLU, has qualified for Million Dollar Round Table membership more than twenty-five times, is the author of numerous articles and books, and is a leading teacher and lecturer nationwide. If anyone knows about tapping sources of extra strength, Frank Sullivan is the person. And he says to feed the spirit.

Scientists and doctors are becoming more and more aware these days of the body's power to heal itself through mental relaxation and the nurturing of inner peace. This is just another form of spiritual growth.

As Christians, we need to be constantly aware of emotional ups and downs that are casually labeled "spirit lifts" or "depressed spirits." Both extremes are dangerous. A strong spirit helps you reach a balance. As the general said, it can help you up after the third knockdown during a bad week or it can inspire us to make a good week even better.

So, the next time you go the extra mile and accomplish something and someone slaps you on the back and says, "Now, that's the spirit!" just wink at the person, smile, and reply, "You don't know how right you are, friend. You just don't know how right you are."

More recently I have been putting together all kinds of information
of the sort of cocoon inhabitance contemporary. I am intrigued
by the vast undertaking and varied pursuit in specific attitude,
for example, in The's day of that - It as it Network, of our
standing, book to flow much adopted conseguences, a final, front.
Lights up as the makes to change the whole type are writing
working a pass right, his and whatever he a keep for attacked
chunk within a simple process, everyone can who has aimed for
CEOs, we incidence not prefer. Rather, and, I die somewhere

into back as the was leaning, feature and customer heights, all
aboves entire about whole we are in the possible, I had think
been a recognition so the whole this for whole can want those
should, i real to know of the whole can pay i comment making those
has in the home planning, the who we has inside a my, remotion
similar greatly.

As for those, we need to be essentially work if supported by
and through it and is watch heedful where late on. Problem at type
with in the cocoon can irregular, As time, that serve you can
a balance. Cocoon is of with if you had he we another the thing
given a during a fashion is a conversations to make a good

A1 does not.

Go the poor inner end to of it, that, intended through a cocon
fund in whatever we depicted and in of but sail. The other
confirmation may wide at the power for has ever try, read don't
as much the pain see me which and can want, feature how related.

**"Cocooning is a
continuous process
of becoming."**

Chapter 3:

Cocooning

A t this point you may be saying to yourself that you feel as though the Holy Spirit is already at work in you; you have personal doubts, however, about whether you will ever be able to see yourself as a highly motivated person capable of a leadership role. If you are thinking such thoughts, you need to be shown how great your potential is—if you will only "see" it in its proper perspective.

The New Testament refers to our salvation experience as being "born again." I like that metaphor because it means we can be dead to our former selves and alive to a new life in Christ (2 Corinthians 5:17).

I am troubled at times, however, because some Christians who say they are "born again" appear to be in an "early grave." Although they breathe, eat, walk, talk and think, they act as though they are in "spiritual neutrality"—they've lost the zest of their Christianity. These people need a lesson in spiritual and personal cocooning. They need to go back deep within themselves and become transformed through the workings of the Holy Spirit and then come out again as something new and beautiful.

If you've seemed spiritually sluggish lately and nonchalant about your outlook on life, you could probably benefit from a bit of cocooning, too. Let me explain how it's done.

Whenever a marketing consultant is brought in to build sales for a business, she first gives the business a new image. She doesn't set about to change the business itself, but merely the way people perceive it.

And it works!

For example, a town may have seven used car dealers, but only one "prior-owned vehicles" dealer; and it's the latter that will attract new customers. A city may have a dozen optical stores, but only one "eye care boutique"; and it's the latter that will get all the youth-oriented business.

Can't you do the same thing? Can't you change your concept of "old age" to "vintage maturity?" "past your prime" to "at the summit?" "youthful inexperience" to "open-minded enthusiasm?"

Of course!

It's all a matter of discovering your strengths and capitalizing on them and admitting your weaknesses and overcoming them. If you don't like the image you are projecting now, you can put yourself into the cocoon of the Holy Spirit and emerge as someone with a totally new image.

The psalmist asked the Lord, "What is man that you are mindful of him?" Within the unspoken response is an assumption that people are special creations, individualized beings capable of accomplishments even admirable in the eyes of the Supreme Being.

If God has given us such talents and individualized abilities, should it not follow that we should discover them within ourselves? They can be used to reshape our image, change our thinking, and give us new vitality.

In the Chinese language, the character drawing for *setback* is the same symbol for "opportunity." That's often true in life, too. Is that upset apple cart a big mess, or did you just discover apple sauce? Is that piece of singed glass a ruined window, or have you just invented sunglasses? It's all in how you perceive things. Pray that God will open your eyes to the innovative opportunities all around you.

How are you presently visualizing yourself? Are you naive about wrinkles, receding hairlines, extra weight, and general grooming that you see in the mirror? Are you visualizing "ghosts" of your former self or are you seeing the real you and then capitalizing on this present self?

Dennis Hensley

Know Thyself

To improve your life, you need an inventory of your bad habits, health weaknesses, and undisciplined behavior patterns so that you will know precisely where to improve. Ask yourself the following questions. Consider your responses carefully. Be honest, frank, objective, and realistic.

1. Am I healthy, energetic, and strong?
2. Do I "think young?"
3. Am I defensive about my appearance?
4. Am I a constant complainer?
5. Do I eat right, sleep enough, and exercise regularly?
6. Do others trust me?
7. Do I act as though I like challenges?
8. Do I show appreciation for the people I work/live with?

Having taken this first step toward knowing more about yourself, you will begin to feel more confident. You can capitalize on this growing confidence if you will use it to become motivated. It wasn't until Jonah was motivated that he journeyed to Nineveh to preach. Once Zacchaeus was motivated, he made amends to those he had cheated.

Part of your cocooning process will be for you to motivate yourself. God has much for you to be doing (Haggai 2:4). You must become motivated, of your own free choice, before you can fulfill your preconceived idea of yourself. Cocooning is a continuous process of becoming. So:

- Become aware of your true potential.
- Become determined to fulfill that potential.
- Become disciplined in pursuing righteous goals.
- Become opportunity-oriented in serving God.
- Become enthusiastic and optimistic about your ambitions.
- Become more knowledgeable in your calling or ministry.

When you develop the power to motivate yourself, you will go a long way in reshaping your image in a positive way. You'll note the difference right away. People who used to think of you as being lazy will now admire your drive. People who previously never asked your advice will now turn to you for your opinions and judgments.

As you receive such trust and positive reinforcement, you will develop more energy. You will discover that your curiosity will increase in proportion to your rising energy. You will desire to learn more about everything and you will discover that you have the energy by which to do the learning.

Be informed on issues related to politics, business, science, ethics, and the arts. Be concerned about global tensions, community affairs, and family needs. Form opinions on such matters as religious freedom, sexual harassment, racial bigotry, environmental pollution, and military preparedness. Unlike the ostrich that buries its head in the sand, you must be alert, informed, and aware of the world around you.

Straight Talk

As you increase your awareness of things, you will want to share your opinions, viewpoints, and ideas with others. Enhance this by altering your mode of talking. Instead of having people continue to think of you as a shrill-toned, idle chatterer, change that image so that they now see you as an even-voiced, well-informed, confident speaker. Here are some tips on how to change your way of talking:

1. Avoid profanity and slang.
2. Increase your vocabulary.
3. Neutralize dialects and accents.
4. Develop a controlled, pleasing tonal quality.
5. Pronounce words clearly and correctly.
6. Speak in complete sentences and at an even pace.
7. Maintain eye contact with the other person.

These speaking-pattern changes will assist you in becoming a more confident and dynamic person. Use your imagination to help you see a strong personal image of yourself to go with your strong, confident voice. Never sell yourself short and never limit your potential for strength and ability. Always strive to see new possibilities in yourself. Maintain a robust faith in your new image, goals, and progress.

Spiritual cocooning can become your fountain of youth. You can use your determination and spiritual strength to revamp your life as often as necessary to keep yourself happy and productive. You may wish to evaluate your life at the end of each calendar year and then plan redirections.

The cocooning process is systematic and dependable. Remember the precedure we have discussed: pray to God for creative wisdom; identify what and who you currently are; decide what new image you would need to project; become self-motivated to achieve this new image; expand your knowledge and awareness of things so that you can capitalize on your new image; and speak and act in ways that properly portray your new image.

All your life you've heard people use that old cliché about getting a new lease on life. With spiritual cocooning, you can make that cliché become reality.

"You simply cannot allow rejection to impede your personal motivation."

Chapter 4:

Overcoming Rejection

Obtaining a new lease on life will not make your life perfect. You will still have to overcome many obstacles and barriers. You'll be rejected by many people. In 1980 President Reagan won the election, but 40,283,488 people voted against him. Did that break his morale? No. He worked hard to prove himself a worthy leader. In 1984 he carried 49 of the 50 states and won easily.

You simply cannot allow rejection to impede your personal motivation. I've learned to cope with this negative aspect of life and so can you. Let me share a secret with you.

I keep a "Humility File" in the back of one of my home office cabinets.

Some of the contents of that file date back to 1967, the first year I entered the field of freelance writing, and others are as recent at last week.

The file is filled with rejection letters.

They are letters from editors of national periodicals who have returned my manuscripts without buying them. Some of the letters are flat and blunt ("We do not accept freelance contributions") and others are syrupy and maudlin ("We very much regret our painstakingly hard decision to refuse your fine manuscript, but . . . ").

The bottom line is the same, however: I invested a lot of time and hard work to research and write an article and then present it in my most professional manner, but I did not gain a sale. I was rejected. I was turned down.

This fact is hard for people who know me to grasp. I run writing workshops and give guest lectures at more than two dozen universities and writing clubs each year. Because my byline has appeared hundreds of times in many of the leading publications in this country, my students think that selling manuscripts is no problem for me. But they are wrong.

The fact is, in freelance writing, as in most selling businesses, each new presentation is judged on its own merits and if it's not what the editor (client) wants, it gets rejected.

And that hurts.

I just hate rejections. I don't care how they are worded—nicely or bluntly—I hate them.

That's probably why I do everything I can to avoid them. And (fortunately) my "Humility File" indicates that I must be on the right track, because I now receive only ten percent as many rejections as I did in 1967. Of course, I did not have the view of rejections then that I have now.

In truth, in 1967 I was about as shallow in my understanding of rejections as a person could be. Let me show you how my naivete held me back.

Job Identity

When I was in my first year of college I got it into my head that I wanted to be a writer. My concept of a writer was that of someone who picked up a notepad, traveled to exotic places, met interesting people, wrote about his or her discoveries, and made a lot of easy money. Years later I learned what a writer really is—someone who bangs on a secondhand typewriter, seldom gets out of town, meets an occasional interesting person, and makes an amount of money in direct proportion to the hours of hard work he or she puts in.

I wasted several good years as I dabbled in journalism, playwriting, and fiction, running into brick walls everywhere as I sought my identity as some kind of a writer.

So, rule one is this: **Understand your job and what it entails, and if you cannot face up to its negative aspects, don't get involved in it.**

Quantity versus Quality

Another problem I had as a beginning freelance writer was that I believed that persistence would be rewarded on its own merit. For two years I wrote manuscripts like a man possessed. I'd write, type, and mail an article a day some of those weeks.

My only rewards for this marathon writing stint were fifty-seven used manila envelopes, several dollars in canceled stamps, sore typing fingers, and the first fifty-seven rejection slips for my "Humility File."

In my third year I learned to study a target publication carefully to determine writing style, audience, article length, editorial guidelines, and use of photos. I also spent more time on my writing. I edited, reviewed, revised, rewrote, and retyped whole pages four or five times. That year my sales more than doubled.

So, rule two is this: **Do your research, prepare a quality presentation, and don't let volume alone form your sales planning.**

Educational Preparation

Perhaps my greatest flaw in my early career days was my belief that anyone could write professionally. After all, I reasoned, I had been writing since second grade. It was simple. In fact, I had talent. My teachers always complimented me on my penmanship and my grandmother was forever telling people that I wrote her lovely letters.

So, I dashed off a couple of short stories and a few articles and waited for my royalty checks to arrive. It was a three-year wait. And I was only successful then because by that time I had taken some college courses in journalism and had read more than thirty books on how to write.

Writing is an art. The more you study it, the better you become at it. Along with that goes the study one must give to the subject being presented.

Rule three, then, is this: **Read, study, and thoroughly research your subject and your sales techniques so that your client will have faith in you.**

Follow-Up

A simple mistake I made as a novice writer was to continually look for new markets. I later learned that once an editor had accepted one of my articles, I had my foot in the door. It was easy to return to a magazine where my writing and research abilities were already established. This saved time, cut red tape, and increased my income quickly.

The same applies to most situations in life. Satisfied people will be far less likely to reject you than will strangers. So keep tabs on your friends, church friends, and relatives and let them encourage you.

Rule four: **Pursue new people but keep in touch with close acquaintances.**

Many times my writing students will lament to me, "I'm beginning to think it's not worth it. There are just too many rejections in this business. It's too hard. Everyone else I talk to has the same problem, too."

To that I get excited and explain, That is what is so wonderful about rejection. This would not be a challenging occupation if the continuous grapple with rejection didn't exist.

Nor would this field be so accessible and lucrative. Sure, everyone gets rejected—even the top pros. But be glad about that. It shows that if you are well prepared, your chance is as strong as anyone's for success!

Whether you are marketing manuscripts, running for public office, selling magazines door to door, or even sharing your personal testimony, you will be faced with rejection. Rejection is part of the process; it is not the end product of your efforts. Keep trying. Don't give up.

Four Rules for Overcoming Rejection

1. Understand your job and what it entails and if you cannot face up to its negative aspects, don't get involved in it.
2. Do your research, prepare a quality presentation and don't let volume alone form your sales planning.
3. Read, study, and thoroughly research your subject and your sales techniques so that your client will have faith in you.
4. Pursue new people but keep in touch with close acquaintances.

> **"The key idea to remember is that everyone who works hard is a potential victim of burnout."**

Chapter 5:

Symptoms and Cures
of Burnout

Does "never give up" mean that life can offer no respite from work? Indeed not. In fact, just as machines need preventative maintenance and "down" times, so do human beings. A machine that runs at full throttle on a nonstop basis will finally burn out its motor. People who have no sense of pace can also burn out. In fact, that can be a problem for people who do not understand the balance between motivation and fanaticism.

We live in a fast world these days. People used to wait three days for a stagecoach. Today, they get upset if they miss one section of a revolving door.

Speed seems to be the primary concern of everyone. Fast-food restaurants, one-hour dry cleaners, high-speed computers, automatic-developing cameras and supersonic transports are routine parts of this whirlwind we call life. Is it any wonder, then, that from time to time we "overload" our mental and physical circuits and cause burnouts?

Have you ever said, "I'm not as excited about life as I want to be?" That's a possible indication of burnout. Have you ever asked, "Why do I always feel so fatigued," or "What! Another church meeting?" or "Who needs that client anyway?" These, too, are possible indications of burnout.

Burnout can sometimes become so advanced that it will manifest physical symptoms, such as insomnia, headaches, backaches, weight loss, nervousness, and exhaustion.

It can also reveal itself in behavioral patterns. For example, executives who increase their rate of absenteeism, lose concern for their clients and prospects, overreact to criticism, or make snap decisions about people, may be suffering from burnout. If left unchecked, this condition can also lead to marital problems, alcoholism, or drug abuse.

To be a successful Christian, you need to have enthusiasm, optimism, individualism, and imagination. Being only human, however, you sometimes find it difficult to maintain a good and constant grip on these four factors. Life is not always manageable. Quite often, you are made to take the bitter with the sour.

Fortunately, if you are wise enough to recognize burnout for what it is, you can also be wise enough to overcome it. Let me offer you ten ways to reverse the feeling of being burned out.

The first two things you need to do are **to get adequate sleep and exercise.** The body requires rest. Don't overtax it. Go to bed a little earlier than usual, take a catnap after supper, and enjoy a long nap on Sunday afternoon. They will give new vitality to your system. Similarly, a brisk half-hour walk at lunchtime plus a couple of evenings of bowling or racketball will add stamina to your physical makeup. If you allow your body to deteriorate, your stress circuits will overload much quicker.

The next two things you need to do are to **make positive uses of your past and future.** You should keep a log of your greatest sales days and key career moments. Read this log frequently and draw encouragement from your past successes. Similarly, get into the habit of always planning something to look forward to and be excited about. Call a close friend and set up a lunch date for next week; arrange a weekend of fishing for early next month; sign up to attend a sales seminar in Hawaii next winter. Plan always to have a future-event "carrot" dangling in front of you.

The fifth tip is to **study something new.** Mental stimulation is a cure-all for both depression and fatigue. Choose a target subject that you have never focused upon previously. Spend a lot of time and energy learning all you can about it: read available articles; listen to a cassette-tape series or read a book about it; talk with people who are knowledgeable about the topic and ask for their views; assemble a file on the subject. By giving yourself a challenge, and by opening a new avenue of interest, you will add zest and spark to your life.

The sixth suggestion is to **learn to say no.** You simply cannot be all things to all people. If you accept more responsibilities than you have time to handle properly, you will generate incredible amounts of worry, frustration, and stress. When you are approached to handle something and you do not have the time to do it, be honest and direct enough to say no. It may be hard at first, but if you constantly remind yourself that it is for your own good, as well as the good of the project you are being drafted into helping, you will soon be able to reject offers without feeling guilty.

A seventh tip is for you to **travel more.** Burnout can sometimes be caused by boredom, which is compounded by a lack of diversity in surroundings. If you've been reporting to the same office or working in the same city for five years, plan a change-of-place. Get out and see new faces, travel new roads, eat in different restaurants. Keep busy with your work, but add some variety for a week. Keep in mind that even in work locales, variety is the spice of life.

An eighth idea is for you to **develop a hobby.** John F. Kennedy used to unwind by reading mystery novels. Winston Churchill found serenity in painting landscapes. Anyone in a challenging job needs to find an avenue of escape from the regular grind. Choose a hobby, such as stamp or coin collecting, gardening, or woodworking that will so totally occupy your concentration that you will be able to put your career in the background for an hour or two. Just as traveling to different locations can be mentally stimulating, so, too, can working on different projects.

A ninth suggestion is to **set realistic and flexible goals** for yourself. Goal-setting is a great idea for anyone. If your goals are not attainable or your time frame is unreasonably demanding, however, you will burn yourself out trying to reach the unreachable. Be a little more compassionate with yourself. Set goals that are challenging, but don't try to become an attorney in two years or try to own your own agency after one year of insurance selling. You don't need that kind of anxiety or frustration.

The final tip is to **set up a support group of friends and peers** who can offer you advice and encouragement. Do this by inviting people with common interests and objectives to a weekly or monthly talk session. Keep the meeting's tone informal, but follow a procedure each time. One meeting can be a social hour and idea exchange session; another meeting can feature a guest speaker who will help the group to overcome a common problem (time management, public relations, sales, or whatever); yet another meeting can be a "confession session" in which each person tells of a personal or business problem currently facing him or her and in which resolution input from the others in the group is offered. These support groups can give you perspective on life, answers to business problems, and opportunities for fellowship.

The key idea to remember is that everyone who works hard is a potential victim of burnout. By incorporating some or all of the previously mentioned ten tips, you can pull yourself out of the burnout doldrums or keep yourself from ever entering a career burnout phase.

Summary

We learned in Part 1 that the key to becoming a great motivator is first to learn how to become self-motivated. God offers us many opportunities for service to him and to other people, as well as opportunities for personal advancement, but God expects us to show some personal initiative, too. We cannot expect to accomplish great things if we remain idle.

The processes for motivating ourselves include maintaining a perspective on life, nurturing the guidance of the Holy Spirit, viewing ourselves in positive ways, learning to overcome rejection, avoiding burnout, and mastering the techniques of problem solving. I suggest you review Part 1 on a regular basis as a way of keeping your motivation level tuned up. Remember that people will be taking their cue from you. If you are fighting the good fight and running the good race, they will feel they can do no less.

"God hath not
given us the spirit
of fear, but of
power, and of love,
and of a sound mind.**"**
2 Timothy 1:7

Chapter 6:

Solving Life's Problems

Before we end this section, I want you to consider some specific procedures that you can use across the board in dealing with any sort of problem that may threaten the momentum of your personal motivation. God has blessed us with a logical mind. It can be used to attack and conquer our problems systematically.

The people I've admired most in the Bible have been the individuals who were the problem solvers. They saw situations of distress or trouble and they used their God-given intelligence to find answers and resolutions to those problems. I've learned a lot about what it takes to be a success in life by studying the behavior of these people.

We all know the story of how Solomon used reverse psychology to discover the real identity of the disputed baby's mother (1 Kings 3:16-27). That story still impresses me.

I also admire the plan Jethro gave Moses for organizing a legal appeals system for the Children of Israel (Exodus 18:17-26). By learning to divide labors and delegate responsibilities, Moses became a better manager of time and a more efficient leader.

David worked out a three-pronged battle strategy to defeat Absalom's greater forces (2 Samuel 18:1-8). Job used logic and analogy to match wits with the four who came to accuse him of sinning. Daniel used a plan of physical discipline and mental agility to outwit the ploys of Nebuchadnezzar (Daniel 1:12-20).

These people were thinkers. They knew something that many of us have forgotten today—we are not serving God when we simply pray for God to do all of our work for us. God works through us, not in place of us.

God wants us to be energetic and bold, strong and confident, assured and eager in all that we do. As Paul wrote, "God hath not given us the spirit of fear, but of power, and of love, and of a sound mind" (2 Timothy 1:7). If the activities we engage in are right in God's eyes, we should have the grit and savvy needed to overcome any problems that arise from these activities.

Problem-solving does not have to be something we automatically toss onto someone else's shoulders. One pastor recently told me, "I am glad to serve as a counselor and advisor to the members of my church, but more than half the problems people bring to me could be solved on their own if people would just use common sense. It often happens that as people begin to explain their problems to me, they also begin to come up with possible solutions. They could have done the same thing at home."

Whereas there are times when we all need help or advice from others, in truth, there are some simple procedures we can learn to follow that will help us solve many of our own problems.

How It's Done

Begin with prayer (Matthew 21:22). Seek the blessing and guidance of the Holy Spirit in all your decision-making procedures. God has granted us free will to express ourselves in the manner of our choice but has also dictated that we exercise responsibility in making use of the talents with which we are blessed. Divine inspiration is still part of the heritage of modern Christianity; equally important, divine sanctification of our personal ideas will give us the confidence needed to follow problems through to their solutions.

Get a complete picture of your problem. Do research; spend time making lists of factors related to your problem; gain a perspective on the total challenge that is before you. Joshua always sent spies into the territory of his enemies before he did battle with them. He would use all the information they brought back to him as guides on how to plan and stage a battle. Before we can do battle against the problems that face us, we need to spy out the extent to which they have spread.

Pinpoint the specific difficulty. Analyze each factor you listed in the previous overview phase of your problem-solving process. Eliminate those items that really are not pertinent to the current problem. Arrange the remaining items according to priorities and concentrate your efforts on the most crucial item. This will give you focus and direction.

Brainstorm about this chief problem. Analyze it from your viewpoint and from other people's viewpoints. Compare the way you are dealing with the problem and the way others are dealing with it. Compare your current success at coping with this problem to the success you had in coping with it one, three, and five years ago. Take into consideration any outside factors (inflation, weather, elections, new laws, new competition) that you may have carelessly ignored until now.

Spend time analyzing yourself in relation to the problem: Are you too old or too young to handle it alone? Too biased to see both sides of the issue? Undereducated or overqualified in dealing with the problem? Do you have a desire to solve the problem successfully or are you annoyed by the tediousness of it? Once you have concentrated on the many aspects of your specific problem, you will have a full range of circumstances and information on which to base your responses.

Sleep on it. Don't be in a hurry to find a quick answer to your problem. Give the analytical half of your brain time to compute the pros and cons of your problem's possible solutions. You can do this subconsciously. Before you begin your normal work day, pull out the notes you jotted down during your brainstorming session and read them over once. At the end of the day, read them again before you go to sleep. In between times, don't worry about making a conscious effort to solve your problem. Instead, each time your subconscious pops a possible solution into your mind, jot it down and save it. Give the subconscious time to analyze the full scope of the problem.

List your options. Keep a running record of all the options that your conscious and subconscious minds present to you. Every problem has a variety of solutions; the key is to select the best one. When the five thousand people who had gathered to hear Christ preach grew hungry, the disciples presented Jesus with a variety of options: the people could be told to stay but remain hungry; the people could be sent home; one boy's lunch could be divided among a few. Christ chose to multiply the little boy's food offering. The disciples had not taken time to come up with the best option.

Solve the problem. Choose what you feel the very best solution to the problem is and get behind it with all your effort to make it work. Press for action, never doubt your ability to succeed, strive for excellent results, and refuse to be satisfied until you get the solution you want. Should you still fail, there will be no shame. You will know you did your best, and you will still be able to pull out your notes and have your other options ready to try. The bottom line in all problem-solving is to never say die. Remember that as a child of God, you are never in the struggle alone.

Part 2

Mental Confidence and Emotional Strength

Have you ever stopped to think that being average means that you are as close to the bottom as you are to the top? You're neither a winner nor a loser.

The motivated, enthusiastic person has a strong desire to be something and uses his or her mind to develop plans for personal development. Thus, we must learn how to maximize the use of our minds before we attempt to develop any other forms of personal advancement.

Ideas may be a dime a dozen, but the people who use them are priceless. A corollary to that statement should be that people who know how to stimulate ideas are even farther ahead of the game. Knowing how to think clearly and logically, to concentrate, to make decisions, and to research your ideas helps you tackle any problem or obstacle before you. A person must think success before he or she can achieve success.

"Too many of us degrade and underrate our abilities to the point that our emphasized humility leads us to feelings of inadequacy. Failure soon follows. It is far better to program ourselves for success."

Chapter 7:

Images of Success

Now-classic studies conducted more than three decades ago by Dr. Maxwell Maltz revealed how important the state of the human mind is to success and motivation. The mind of a human being has a powerful element that the minds of lesser beings do not possess: imagination. With it, a person can become a creator—of art, music, and poetry, and of machinery, corporate structures, and business strategies.

Maltz's psycho-cybernetics studies revealed that the human central nervous system is incapable of distinguishing between real and imagined situations. For example, if a person dreams that she is being chased by a bear, she begins to breathe rapidly and perspire, just as though the event were real. A nightmare is often a very terrifying "real" event.

Maltz noted, however, that the imagination could also be used for positive image building. If the mind could vicariously experience a successful speech or a successful sale or a successful trip to the batter's box, and if the mind could replay these scenes of success often enough, they would become as convincingly real from a positive perspective as the nightmare had been from a negative perspective.

It is by conscious, rational thought that our subconscious thoughts and reactions can be changed. Our decisions, actions, and emotions are reactions to our beliefs. Whatever our minds believe to be true will be true to the rest of our bodily functions. If our minds tell us that we are great orators, however, we will remain calm and in control when we appear before a crowd. Conversely, if our minds tell us that we are poor orators, we will experience racing hearts, moist palms and foreheads, and stammering speech. In this sense truth is what we perceive truth to be.

Mental Programming

Mental practice makes perfect. It is not arrogance or egotism to imagine ourselves in a successful mode. Too many of us degrade and underrate our abilities to the point that our emphasized humility leads us to feelings of inadequacy. Failure soon follows. It is far better to program ourselves for success.

The mental programming for success that we need to undertake can be thought of as serious make-believe. It is like the make-believe games we used to play as children in which we pictured ourselves as knights, cowboys, soldiers, nurses, fashion models, or schoolteachers. This time, however, the game is for real. This time, when we imagine ourselves as millionaires, athletic champions, valedictorians, top salespeople, or company presidents, we will not later erase the image.

Our success image is not something we can be nonchalant about; we must treat it seriously. Rather than daydream from time to time, or hope to be the new manager, we should visualize ourselves in that role. We should consider such things as what we will wear, what we will say, and what we will be in control of. The more precise we can be in our visualizations, the more real these roles will become to us. The more real they become, the faster we will be drawn to them.

Positive thoughts produce results. If you act like a success, others will perceive you to be a success. Envision only victory. Remember that success attracts success.

If you are optimistic, you will find yourself able to cope with virtually any situation. From John Milton's *Paradise Lost* comes the adage, "The mind is its own place, and in itself can make a Heav'n of Hell, a Hell of Heav'n." Abraham Lincoln stated it more simply: "Most people are about as happy as they make up their minds to be."

How can we be happy? By putting our minds at ease. And how

is this done? Through common sense behavior: don't worry about things you cannot control; react calmly and levelheadedly during times of crisis; feel and act happy; treat other people warmly; and behave as though your continued success is inevitable.

**////I have the power
to conquer anything
if I believe in myself,
maintain an earnest
concentration on the
problem, and devote
time every day to
meeting the challenge.////**

Chapter 8:

Controlling Anxiety

Anxiety is one of the greatest factors in undermining enthusiasm. You cannot behave like a highly motivated person if you are burdened with guilt, fear, confusion, or tension.

You can only come to grips with feelings of anxiety by confronting them. My suggestions are these:

- Through prayer seek God's wisdom in your considerations.
- After an honest evaluation of a negative situation, decide if there is really any logical reason for your distress.
- If your anxiety is exaggerated, put it into its proper perspective or forget it completely.
- If your anxiety is legitimate, remind yourself that you can find a solution to your problem if you stay calm and use your creative problem-solving talents.

Probably nothing will serve you better in overcoming negative mental attitudes than the ability to believe in yourself and your capabilities. If you can foster this self-confidence, you can do almost anything.

Why Belief Is Important

Several years ago, I learned a simple, but powerful object lesson about the power of belief. A seemingly minor incident has had an ongoing impact on my life. It taught me that I must have complete confidence in myself if I am to succeed at whatever I do.

At the time, my youngest brother-in-law Tim was still in high school and living with his parents. One day Tim and I happened to be watching television together. A talk-show guest was showing the audience how to juggle. Tim listened intently and then ran to find three tennis balls to practice with. I grew bored with it all, however.

When the show ended, Tim attempted to follow the juggler's instructions. He even made me stand up and try it a few times. The tennis balls bounced around the living room. I felt foolish, and Tim—arms flailing in the air—looked silly to me.

"Forget it," I said. "That stuff's for circus performers. Guys like us are too old to master something like that. You probably have to start practicing when you're a kid."

Undaunted, Tim went off to his bedroom to continue his practicing. During the rest of our visit, I laughed every time I heard the tennis balls bouncing off the walls and furniture.

About two weeks later, Tim came by to see my wife and me. He brought along three tennis balls.

"Look at this," he said proudly. He tossed the tennis balls into the air and juggled them for five full rotations before dropping them. "Not bad, eh? I'm really getting better. A little more practice, and I'll have it down pat."

I was amazed. He could actually do it. I had told him it was impossible, but he had believed it was possible. And his belief had made it possible. He had mastered juggling.

Suddenly, something occurred to me: if this gangly high-school kid could learn to juggle, I knew good and well that I could, too—if I set my mind to it.

I was not about to let some awkward young kid show me up. I promised myself that I would learn to juggle or die trying. It became an obsession with me. I bought tennis balls and practiced every day. At night I lay in bed and mentally rehearsed the movements—the timing, the pitches, and the catches.

A week later, I could do two full rotations. In two weeks, I could juggle for three minutes before dropping the balls. In three weeks, I could juggle as long as I wanted to.

After one month's time, I had gone from thinking that I could never learn to juggle to being able to juggle in a simple cascade motion, in an over-the-top cascade, and even in a forehand forward-grab rotation. What caused this advancement? Two things: motivation (I just couldn't let my little brother-in-law show me up) and belief (the knowledge that if Tim could learn to juggle, so could I).

Since then, whenever I have been confronted by a task that seemed impossible, I have remembered the juggling episode. I've reminded myself of the power I have to conquer anything if I believe in myself, maintain an earnest concentration on the problem, and devote time every day to meeting the challenge. As I noted before, mental practice does make perfect. Along with that, belief is indispensable.

Chapter 9:

Belief and Motivation

It is impossible to separate belief from motivation. One cannot have a driving belief in something without being motivated by that belief. Similarly, one cannot be greatly motivated without believing in something. But what are the elements that can create a belief, a confidence in ourselves? In my experience, several of those elements have been these:

1. **Clear Conscience:** You must feel that what you are about to engage in is within the ethical, moral, professional, and social codes of your personal convictions, and that the job you undertake will measure up to your personal standards of honesty, fairness, and trust. If the work does not meet these criteria, you will find yourself resisting it and struggling against it.

2. **Adequate Knowledge:** You must feel that you either have—or will be able to obtain—the needed instruction, training, and experience to handle the task at hand. If you feel that you are inadequately prepared for the work, you will be hesitant in your actions, slow with your decisions, and overly cautious about your recommendation.

3. **Worthwhile Mission:** You must be convinced that the task you are about to accept is a worthy job, in the sense that it will make some sort of positive contribution to yourself, your family, your church, your business, or society itself. More than likely, you will not be motivated by salary alone. We all need to feel that our lives are being used for something worthwhile.

4. **Potential Advancement:** You must be convinced that once you

complete the job or master the skill, you will be better off because of it. If the successful completion of your goal does not reward you with a social, economic, or personal prize, you will be hard-pressed to justify why you should be involved in it. Christians like to feel they are "laying up treasures in heaven."

If your situation encompasses the previous four elements, your belief will be strong in whatever you attempt to do. This belief will drive you on to success. As Dr. Charles Mayo observed, "No man ever died from overwork, but many died from doubt."

People with confidence and belief are motivated and eager to face their challenges. They have boundless energy. They are life's positive workaholics, the leaders who have the mental stability and creativity to push their churches, corporations, shops, or firms to the top.

You know how to formulate a positive mental image of yourself, the same way other leaders do. Use that skill. In fact, use every aspect of the power your mind has to offer.

Chapter 10:

Enthusiasm and Skill

Enthusiasm makes the difference between just doing a job and doing a job well. But no amount of enthusiasm or motivation can make up for a lack of basic business-related skills. In fact, the full potential of enthusiasm can only be realized when it is applied to mastering the activities required by the work you do.

Thomas Wolfe wrote, "If a man has talent and cannot use it, he has failed. If he has a talent and uses only half of it, he has partly failed. If he has a talent and learns somehow to use the whole of it, he has gloriously succeeded, and won a satisfaction and a triumph few men ever know." Through enthusiasm you will learn how to use the whole of your talent, your skills, and win the success you desire.

Famed psychologist Sir William James advised, "Believe that life is worth living and your belief will help create the fact." Belief begins in the mind. Enthusiasm and motivation are stimulated by confidence and belief in one's mission in life. Belief then must be combined with skill to achieve success.

〰〰〰〰〰〰〰〰〰〰〰〰〰〰〰〰〰〰〰〰〰〰

"Successful decision makers are people who seek a decision that will be most beneficial for themselves and for the people upon whom the decision will impact."

〰〰〰〰〰〰〰〰〰〰〰〰〰〰〰〰〰〰〰〰〰〰

Chapter 11:

Decision Making

Having mastered the ability to envision yourself as a dynamic leader, you must also learn how to use the power of your mind for a variety of leadership-related activities. Let's look first at the process of decision making.

One of the most challenging mental tasks any of us has to face is making a decision. The process becomes even more agonizing when the fate of other people is riding on our choices and rulings. The anxiety can often be so unbearable that many people refuse to make a decision at all. Of course, choosing not to decide is, itself, a decision. (And, I might add, a poor one.)

There are many people who claim to thrive on decision making. It makes them feel powerful and in control. These positive feelings remain as long as the decisions are solid and wise. Not all decisions are, however.

Snap decisions are reflex actions and should be avoided. The full consequences of hastily determined conclusions are usually not realized until it is too late to reverse them.

Alternative decisions—choosing among several possible courses of action—need to be faced, whether bad or good. Suppose, for example, you must decide whether to sell one of your factories or fire thirty-five of your senior employees. It's a no-win situation, but if you ignore it, you will eventually lose both the factory and the workers. So, a decision must be made at the time of crisis.

Successful decision makers are people who seek to reach a decision that will be most beneficial for themselves and for the people upon whom the decision will impact. They know that there are only two possible answers to the decision at hand: yes or no. Conversely, however, a limitless range of questions could have a bearing on the decision. Successful decision makers seek the appropriate questions. They consult their managers, colleagues, employees, pastors, and other appropriate people. From them, they acquire a variety of viewpoints, which ultimately lead to questions such as these:

- Is what we are doing God honoring?
- Will we need additional personnel or training?
- What equipment, storage space, and inventory will we need?
- How will we handle advertising, marketing, and distribution?
- What about returns, breakage, insurance, quantity discounts, and delivery?
- How will we handle financing, bookkeeping, and pricing?
- Who are our competitors and what are they offering?

Having obtained a list of questions from a wide variety of people, you must next sort out which questions are specifically applicable to the current decisions. Keep yourself open to questions, ideas, and information that may be contrary to your own feelings and opinions. Your objective is to be aware of the total picture. Since the ramifications of your decision will affect many and last a long time, you must be open to all views and perspectives.

As you focus on answering the questions, you will mentally be making checkmarks on the pro and con sides of the decision. After a period of summary reflection, you will be able to make your decision in view of which side is most heavily weighted. Of course, one's "gut" instinct or intuition will at times be worth heeding, too. But generally speaking, logic and factual analysis about important decision-making will be your strongest considerations.

Chapter 12:

Concentration

Ralph Waldo Emerson noted, "Concentration is the secret of success in politics, in war, in trade; in short, in all the management of human affairs."
The ability to concentrate intently on a matter is one of the key aspects of personal motivation. The person who can concentrate on a project will also be capable of contemplating its successful completion. And anyone who can "see" victory ahead will be eager to pursue the mark.

Concentration is a valuable mental skill that should be cultivated by all success-seeking people. Intense concentration is an acquired talent. We all have the power to concentrate. More importantly, we all have the ability to enhance this capability greatly.

The ability to lose oneself in deep concentration is a skill few people ever fully master. Those who do are seldom understood by others. According to popular legend, when Albert Einstein was developing his most advanced mathematical equations and theories, he often dressed in a most bizarre fashion, wearing socks of different colors, a sweater vest atop a pullover sweater, and tennis shoes with a dress coat. It wasn't that he purposely desired to look eccentric; his thoughts were so deeply focused on his work that he had "no thoughts" for routine matters.

Einstein's accomplishments were incredible. Nevertheless, the world would be in chaos if everyone were lost in intense concentration on one topic the way Einstein was. What is of more practical value to you is the ability to turn on an intensity of concentration whenever it is needed to solve problems, develop ideas, or formulate game plan strategies.

There may be any number of reasons why you have not developed good concentration habits already. You may have had to contend with noise, visual distractions, or stress. I have found that it is best to deal with disruptive matters in direct ways:

- For noise: close your door; disconnect your phone or have your calls held; create "white noise" with an FM radio, humming fan, or dehumidifier; use earplugs; work at the library.
- For clutter: work on a cleared desk; focus on one task at a time; remove family pictures or anything that might cause you to daydream; open one folder at a time, as needed.
- For interruption control: use and enforce "Do Not Disturb" signs; schedule private time each day.

Concentration is enhanced in a variety of ways. The more factors you are able to have working in your favor, the greater the odds that your concentration will be improved. Strive for:

1. A quiet environment
2. Advance organization of time and materials
3. Belief in the value of the job at hand
4. Proper frame of mind
5. Determination and perseverance
6. Anticipation of the current challenge
7. Confidence in yourself
8. Suitable reward for completing the job
9. Curiosity about new approaches to old problems

As we have already noted, your mind is your greatest work asset. The more you can discipline it to concentrate on problems, the more you will be able to capitalize on it.

Having mastered concentration techniques, your next challenge will be to go beyond mere problem-solving. The next level of thinking is to express creativity in concepts. You will attempt to come up with a completely new product, procedure, service, idea, or activity.

Chapter 13:

Stimulating Creativity

I teach dozens of writing seminars each year. Many of my students say, "I just don't know how creative writers do it. Time and again, they come up with new plots, new characters, and even new ways to use the language. They must be gifted."

If these people could have seen the pile of rejection slips I accumulated during the years I was first struggling to get published, they would realize that a creative "gift" takes a long time to develop. Most creative writers will admit that they are not gifted. They are simply people who, through years of practice, have learned how to stimulate creativity.

I'm convinced the same talent has been developed in many church leaders and business people. But these people display their talents as creative righters, rather than writers. Whenever something goes wrong—attendance is low, sales decline, cash flow dries up, the competition gets the edge—and a solution is needed to set things right, the creative righters are always the ones called upon to handle the situation.

Creative righters know how to play with symbols, ideas, names, and numbers to produce a fresh concept. While no one can create something out of a void, it is also true that the reservoir of stored experiences locked in our memories can be forced to the surface to give us current perspectives on the task at hand.

We have a wealth of experiences—the books we've read, TV shows we've seen, conversations we've had, places we've visited, and so on. If all of this can be tapped, there is no end to the new

concepts that can be formulated. Creative righters know how to
go about tapping these resources.

The successful techniques and procedures that I've observed in
creative thinking are these:

1. Go against the grain. All successful creative thinkers dare to
buck tradition. They contemplate radical thoughts. Copernicus
wondered, What if the earth isn't the center of the universe?
Columbus wondered, But what if the earth isn't flat? More
recently, others have considered such outrageous possibilities as
space flight and transplanting the human heart.

Daring to ask the nontraditional question leads the thinker to
the next step: discovering how to make the impossible possible.
This leads to new areas of investigation, new questions to ask.
And that's creativity.

2. Don't fear mistakes. The only people who never make mistakes are the people who never try anything. Thomas Edison once
noted that he "failed his way to success." He experimented with
many different ways to solve a problem or make a new product
work. By keeping at it until, as he put it, he "ran out of mistakes,"
he eventually found the solution.

I believe that all successful creative thinkers have this same attitude. They are so enthusiastic about finding the answer that they
aren't thrown off by temporary setbacks. In fact, for many of
them, trial and error is the most enjoyable part of the creative
process.

3. Mix apples and oranges. Creative thinkers are nosy. They
are always snooping into other people's professions to see what
they can adapt to their own. They try other jobs, read books in
professional fields other than their own, attend seminars on off-
beat subjects, and strike up conversations with experts in numerous professions. Many times, creative thinkers discover an innova-
tion in one field that can be modified slightly to solve a problem in
a different area.

Creative borrowing has been going on for ages. Automobile
safety experts borrowed seatbelts and shatter-proof glass from
aviation experts. Prefabricated home builders borrowed the concept of interlocking house sections from the assembly line procedure at automobile plants. Truly creative thinkers put no blinders
on their research.

4. Brainstorm the illogical. With no limitations or fetters on his or her thinking, the creative person looks at existing practices and tries to imagine how they might be changed. Sometimes, the immediate ideas seem illogical, but the creative thinker considers them, anyway. For example, the obvious regarding air travel in the days of the Wright Brothers was that a flying apparatus had to be lighter than air, such as a hot-air balloon. The Wrights, however, created a heavier-than-air apparatus that used torque and thrust to keep it aloft. It was illogical for the times. But when it worked, the old logic was changed.

5. Believe in your creative capabilities. Creative writers trust their imaginations and analytical talents. They don't give up before they get started. They know that the mind combines conscious study and subconscious analysis in developing new concepts. The process takes time. Just as a computer is given data, then allowed time to search its memory banks for answers, the brain needs time to search for and formulate its references into logical responses. Have faith in yourself. You can be just as creative as anyone else if you'll just take the time to explore all your thought processes.

Summary

Having mastered the skills of self-confidence, we examined further how the mind can be aided in the processes of decision making and concentration. We discovered ways in which the mind can be used to enhance our creative capabilities.

The mind of the highly motivated person is goal oriented, disciplined, creative, analytical, artistic, and self-confident as the result of diligence and practice. You now know the necessary techniques and systems for developing your mind along these lines. It is up to you to apply the practice of these techniques and systems.

"The person who can remain steady during a time of chaos will survive with the least amount of harm and will be the one who can be relied on when the next crisis arises."

53

Part 3
Emotional Control
for Leaders

During World War II, President Roosevelt kept a firm hand on the potential hysteria of the country by warning the people, "We have nothing to fear but fear itself."

Roosevelt had endured every form of personal disappointment—from unsuccessful election campaigns to a crippling attack of polio—and had learned that brooding and worrying accomplished nothing. Victory in politics, business, and war went to those who were able to remain calm and clear-headed. Panic was the worst form of weakness. Emotional control led to rational thinking, and rational thinking led to victory.

These same rules apply to the Christian leader. The person who can remain steady during a time of chaos will survive with the least amount of harm and will be the one who can be relied on when the next crisis arises.

Because leaders must, by necessity, make procedural changes, initiate new systems, and break new ground, they quite often are open to criticism from people who do not understand the whole picture. When ministers or company presidents or other leaders begin to exercise the responsibility of leadership, feathers often get ruffled.

"Why can't she just let well enough alone?" someone will complain.

"Who does that hot shot think he is, trying to tell me how to be more productive!"

"What? A change in our work hours? I hate this! I won't go along with it!"

Such complaints from employees, colleagues, and clients can bring out the worst in business leaders, unless they have learned how to control their emotional reactions. That is what we will be focusing on in this part: how to control our emotions so that we respond, instead of react.

The most potentially dangerous of all emotions is anger. There are times when anger can be an appropriate response. Society, for example, has a right to be angered by vandalism, drunk driving, and corruption in politics. This anger is expressed and vented rationally, however, through legislation and the appointment of public officials to oversee the legal process. These are examples of emotional control at its finest level.

Christ, too, set a good example when he answered questions of those who confronted him and did so with kindness rather than a sharp tongue.

Our control over our individual bouts of anger is usually less disciplined. Quite frankly, we don't like people to upset us. When they do, our instinctive reaction is to "get even."

Chapter 14:

Dealing with Anger

P eople deal with anger in a variety of ways—some positive, some negative. I do not need to spend time explaining why reactions such as screaming, making threats, giving the silent treatment, or passively accepting all blame for an incident are negative ways of dealing with anger. Instead, let's focus on ways to cope with anger.

First, there is what I call vicarious viciousness. This involves venting your anger in ways other than attacking the person or circumstances you are angry with. For example, if you are angry at yourself for some mistake you have made, it would probably help if you went out in your yard and kicked a football several times. Vigorous physical activity is exceptionally good for diminishing anger.

Abraham Lincoln had many political enemies who did their best to thwart his plans to abolish slavery, preserve the union, and increase overseas trade. Lincoln had to work with these bullheaded people, cajoling and persuading until he obtained their cooperation. As an outlet for the anger he frequently experienced, Lincoln made it a practice to sit down and write very harsh letters to these people, in which he insulted, ridiculed, and even threatened them. Then he would burn the letters. Just venting his anger in this vicarious way helped him stay in control of his emotions.

A second way to handle anger is by rerouting it. If, for example, your pet project collapses, immediately turn your frustration and anger to a new project. "I can't believe my partners wouldn't go along with my idea of opening a branch office in Millersburg. All right, then, I'll just have to start landing more sales in Millersburg, so that they can see the potential there. That's my new goal!"

A third way to handle anger is through courteous confrontation. This requires that you control your temper, yet insist your rights not be violated. "I appreciate the problems you've had with bad weather and slow delivery dates for materials, Mr. Williams, but according to the contract we signed, you are to build my new garage for four thousand dollars. That's the amount I will be paying. Cost overruns are your responsibility, I'm afraid."

Controlling anger is something we all must work at diligently. If you anger more easily than most people, admit it—and do something about it. You might begin by carrying a notebook with you for a week. Jot down those things that cause you to become angry. Correct the minor ones: "Marie, you've been late every morning this week. Please try to arrive no later than 8:00 A.M. from now on." Diffuse the major ones: schedule a handball game for immediately after a meeting with your most irksome client.

Anger is a natural human response to negative circumstances. By channeling its unleashed powers in positive directions, not only can it be controlled, but it can also be made useful. Proverbs 15:18 teaches, "A hot-tempered man stirs up strife, but he who is slow to anger quiets contention."

Chapter 15:

Battling the Blahs

Anything can become routine, mundane, dull, and boring if a person has to deal with it for any extended length of time. When the novelty or challenge of an item, event, or situation wears off, boredom sets in. Boredom as a persistent emotional condition can lead to severe depression, lack of productivity, and sometimes even such radical responses as drug dependence, divorce, or suicide. Chronic boredom should not be ignored or treated lightly.

We all must contend with occasional cases of temporary boredom: a lecture we are required to attend; a "conversationalist" who buttonholes us at a party; a fashion show or ball game our spouse has wanted to see. Boring situations are a part of life. They are unavoidable, and so we resign ourselves to them, endure them temporarily, and then seize our opportunity to escape as soon as possible.

Chronic boredom, however, provides no escape. It stays with its victim around the clock. It smothers enthusiasm, stifles imagination, and saps personal energy.

People generally strive to create stability in their lives. There's nothing wrong with this, as long as stability is not equated with tedium. For example, stability is having a job to go to. Tedium is going to that job at the same time, by the same route, 240 times a year. Ho-hum. That's probably why, after the energy crisis abated in 1979, many people continued to go to work in car pools. They had discovered the different cars and morning conversations to be nice changes of pace.

Chronic boredom can have many serious effects on a person's business life:

- Instead of being participants, bored people become spectators.
- Rather than risk failing at something, bored people make excuses for not becoming involved in new projects. Instead of striving to reach goals, the bored person gives up.
- Instead of cooperating, the bored person criticizes, argues with, avoids, and resents all colleagues.

In order to avoid boredom and stay motivated, the business leader must provide a more stimulating and fascinating life for himself or herself. Here are some ways in which I have found this can be accomplished:

1. **Always be involved in some form of study.** Learning new things keeps the mind agile and stimulates creativity. So, register for a seminar on Chinese cooking, sign up for a correspondence course in creative writing, or go to the library and check out five books on time management. Continually challenge your mind to grow.

2. **Regularly take calculated risks.** Break out of the comfort zone by setting your sales goals a little higher than usual, by promising delivery dates a little earlier than is routine, or by agreeing to teach a Sunday school class to people much younger or much older than you. Don't allow yourself to become casual about life or business. Complacency can be numbing.

3. **Keep physically fit.** If you are coping with boredom by snacking, substitute games or exercise for food.

4. **Try a change-of-pace activity.** Attend a weekend puppet festival, try go-carting, tour a doll museum, eat at an East Indian restaurant, or visit a wildlife preserve. There's a fascinating world out there waiting to be discovered.

5. **Change your appearance.** Why not? Try a new hairstyle. Shave your mustache and see if anyone notices. You can try a little variety; you're not cast in steel.

6. **Schedule a private pep rally.** Try to arrange a free hour a few times each week so that you can listen to motivational tapes or view motivational video presentations. Not only will you learn some new and important business concepts, but you'll also rekindle

your competitive fires. And don't forget to maintain your time for daily devotions.

Boredom, like failure, is self-inflicted. It is an avoidable emotional state. The enthusiastic leader will avoid it.

A Test for Boredom

Answer each of the following questions with a yes or no response and then calculate your score according to the table at the bottom of the page.

1. Have I purposely provoked an argument lately?
2. Do I rely on old clients rather than seek new ones?
3. Do I arrive late or leave early from the office?
4. Have I started to eat more lately?
5. Have I displayed any tendency toward violence recently?
6. Do I frequently consider the idea of changing companies?
7. Do I wish we'd had another baby after all?
8. Do I wish I had married someone else?
9. Do I involve myself in a constant flurry of activity so that I don't have time to consider whether I'm bored or not?
10. Have I started to go to bed earlier and take more naps?
11. Do I use aspirin, Valium, diet pills, or other drugs frequently?
12. Have I tried to shock my senses recently?
13. Do I have a constant sense of fatigue or lethargy?
14. Do I display an elitist attitude in which I disdain to become involved in new projects?
15. Do I constantly try to please others rather than myself?

SCORE: How many questions did you respond yes to?

1-3 Your life is still stimulating.
4-6 You are an enthusiastic person, but your job or home environment is not providing the level of enjoyment and stimulation you feel you need.
7-10 You have entered the development stage of chronic emotional boredom.
11-15 You are a victim of chronic boredom and are in need of help from a minister, physician, or counselor.

❝Moses said to the Lord,
'O Lord, I have never
been eloquent, neither in
the past nor since you
have spoken to your
servant. I am slow
of speech and tongue.**❞**
—Exodus 4:10

Chapter 16:

Overcoming Shyness

Have you ever "postponed" an opportunity to witness because you felt shy and self-conscious? Have you ever turned down an invitation to a church activity because you felt shy and hesitant about being around new people? Maybe it's time you learned how to overcome this outreach barrier.

Shyness isn't something just discovered in recent years. People have suffered from it since ancient times—partly because the problem was so often ignored or passed off lightly.

"What? Shy? My wife? She's just a little moody, that's all."

"Yeah, I know my boy's bashful. No big deal. The kid'll come out of his shell when he gets older."

"My daughter is shy, eh? So, who cares? Little girls are supposed to be coy, right?"

Those responses are naive. The truth is that words such as **shyness** and **bashfulness** are just a cover for the real problem: fear. Many experts believe that shy people are genuinely afraid of something.

Their fears can be real or imagined. And the sad irony is that Christians are often among the shyest of people. They read Scripture passages about walking through the valley of the shadow of death and fearing no evil, yet refuse to go out on calling night because they're afraid to face strangers.

Often our fears become stronger than our faith, and we miss opportunities to receive spiritual gifts from God. When God called Moses to speak to pharaoh, Moses complained that he was not eloquent enough to handle the job. His complaining angered the Lord (Exodus 4:14).

"I will be thy mouth and teach thee what thou shalt say," God promised Moses. But Moses lacked faith. As a result, his brother Aaron became God's spokesperson. Moses had a chance to receive the gift of spiritually inspired oratory (1 Corinthians 12:8), but his shyness and fear made him forfeit this blessing.

Religious and lay counselors agree that shyness hasn't been taken seriously enough. It can become an excuse for lack of assertiveness in individuals with poor work records, both in their church and secular jobs. But it can be dealt with if people truly have a desire to overcome it.

"When it comes to overcoming shyness, everything comes down to attitude and preparation," says Dr. L. Stanley Wenck, psychology professor at Ball State University. "People who anticipate that they are going to behave awkwardly around other people actually program themselves to behave that way. Instead, they should develop an attitude of confidence."

Dr. Wenck works with college freshmen living away from home for the first time who feel shy because of their new surroundings. The tips he gives these young adults are useful to any person facing shyness.

"Just as shyness compounds itself, so too does confidence," explains Dr. Wenck. "Shy people should build their confidence in small but steady doses. They can begin by approaching friendly people (a reference librarian, a bank teller, a minister) and asking for advice or help on some matter. Each week they can get to know more and more such people."

He adds, "They also should become members of small groups or clubs where they can be with a few people and not be overwhelmed by a large crowd." Church youth groups and school clubs can help shy teens become more self-assured.

Dr. Wenck admits that strange new surroundings and major life changes such as getting married, going into the military, or going to college, can cause the sort of anxiety that might lead to shyness in people. But that doesn't have to be the case.

"New situations offer as much opportunity for positive things to occur as they do negative things," says Dr. Wenck. "Maybe someone has been hesitant in other situations. Who cares? This is now. Strangers have no preconceived notions about people they meet. If the shy person will behave with confidence, he or she will be accepted as a capable and strong individual. It's a chance to start a new, more assertive life."

Pastors, psychiatrists, and other counselors generally agree that there is nothing baffling or mystical about overcoming shyness. Basically, counselors suggest five procedures to people seeking help:

- **Be yourself.** You have many unique and wonderful God-given personality traits that will attract people to you if you relax and behave naturally (Hebrews 13:5).
- **Don't exaggerate circumstances.** Don't develop needless anxiety about what may happen or what folks might think about you. These are manufactured worries. Keep your negative imaginings under control (Matthew 6:25).
- **Be friendly.** You can find many new friends by first being friendly yourself. A simple handshake, a kind word, and a warm smile go a long way in increasing social contacts for yourself (2 Chronicles 10:7).
- **Get a new view of yourself.** Learn to view your shortcomings as unique aspects of your character. No one except Jesus is perfect; nevertheless, everyone is unique. Capitalize on that (2 Timothy 1:7).
- **Build confidence daily.** Try to accomplish something each day that will expand your circle of friends or expose you to new circumstances. Bite off a little at a time. Progress, no matter how slow or how small, is better than standing still or regressing (James 1:2-3).

God built into us some character elements that enable us to be properly cautious and logically careful. But God didn't create us to be shy wallflowers who sit idly, eyes lowered, in back pews while others work and witness.

Instead, we need to overcome bashfulness to be strong witnesses for Christ. Bashfulness is a problem we should not shy away from (Isaiah 41:10).

Summary

In this part, we have examined the fact that people react to situations in life by displaying emotions. The range of these emotions is great—from fear to bravery, from shyness to anger, from terror to annoyance. Emotions can and should be disciplined and channeled. We looked at ways in which this may be accomplished. We noted that many emotional problems—most notably, shyness—are rooted in fear. The enthusiastic worker must learn to conquer such fears.

Part 4:

Motivating Other People

I n our previous chapters we have focused on how you can motivate yourself to reach new levels of personal success and how these factors of motivation can also prepare you for leadership roles in your church, family, community, or on the job. Ironically, the fact that you now know what to do to become successful will not also guarantee that you will know when to use these skills. Simply stated, the answer to the question of when to use your skills is this: always.

Some people get off to a good start at motivating themselves and others. Later, however, when they are just about to reach their goals and become successful, they pull back. These people are unable to cope with what they perceive to be the "terror of success." To be a great leader, you must not let this thwart your efforts; similarly, you must learn how to help others overcome this imaginary terror.

**"Presuccess anxiety,
whether real or imagined,
exaggerated or correct,
keeps hundreds of people
in all walks of life
from reaching their
full potential."**

Chapter 17:

Coping with Success

Have you ever wondered why some people often run from success when at last it seems so close to them? Even the Bible is filled with such people. After God promised to make Moses a strong spokesperson before pharaoh, Moses shied away and let the gift of oratory go to Aaron. After the Children of Israel reached the border of the Promised Land, they refused to cross over into it. After Christ proclaimed that he would build his church upon Peter's confession, that same Peter denied Christ three times.

In truth, success can sometimes be so terrifying we choose to flee from it. Avoid success? At first, it may seem ludicrous even to consider such a situation. Upon closer examination, however, we find that the fear of success can take two forms: presuccess anxiety, in which a person is so fearful of succeeding he or she does something to prevent it, and success-status guilt, in which a person who has achieved success cannot cope with it.

Christ taught us to be successful in all that we do. He wants us to be committed to excellence, not content with mediocrity. Success, however, must be defined first by peace of mind. Jesus did not criticize Zacchaeus for being wealthy, but he showed him that his wealth would never give him the peace of mind he was seeking. Similarly, Jesus did not criticize Peter, James, and Matthew for being fishermen and a tax collector; he merely called them to something more challenging and demanding.

How about you? Do you have the talent and opportunity to be successful, yet perhaps lack the grit and determination to accept it?

Let's take a moment to see why this may be so and how you can deal with it.

Some people are guilty of self-sabotage. It happens like this: just as a person is about to be promoted or about to win a sales contest, he or she will suddenly become ill and will miss a week of work, or will purposely do something to aggravate the boss, or will even turn in a resignation.

It doesn't make sense, does it? Looking from the outside, perhaps not. But from the inside, it has a logic all its own. In doing research for several years on this subject, I have logged more than fifty so-called "good reasons" people had for thwarting their own success.

- "If I won the sales contest once, I'd be expected to win it again."
- "If I got promoted and my older sister didn't, she would be humiliated."
- "If I accepted the new position, I would have to transfer to Detroit, and I'm terrified of big cities."

Such presuccess anxiety, whether real or imagined, exaggerated or correct, keeps hundreds of people in all walks of life from reaching their full potential.

Equally as damaging is success-status guilt that can often cause a person to topple himself or herself from a position of success after working years to get there. Sometimes, the memories of what was done in the struggle to attain success prove so embarrassing or confusing, feelings of guilt or self-doubt arise.

One man shared with me, "I was given the Outstanding Teacher award in my state, but I can't forget that I broke by mother's heart when I didn't become a doctor."

A woman told me, "In college I bragged that I was going to become a famous portrait artist, but then I had a chance to become an ad designer with a major magazine. So, now I'm rolling in money, but I still feel like a failure."

Handling Success

There are several ways in which "fearful" Christians can learn to cope with and accept success:

1. If your success had been attained by the violation of any of

God's laws, seek God's forgiveness, correct your ways, and make restitution to those you've hurt or alienated. If you feel you cannot handle this alone, seek the help and guidance of a pastoral counselor (Proverbs 15:16).

2. Discard guilt over situations out of your control. If you were promoted because you were better qualified than your sister, it was your employer's choice, not yours. You cannot hold yourself responsible for your employer's needs or your sister's limitations. Just be gracious in your new status. Love conquers all.

3. Remind yourself that as you mature, your goals will change. Maybe you now **prefer** to be an ad designer rather than a portrait painter. Fine! Both are legitimate and worthy occupations. It's your life, remember (Ecclesiastes 7:8).

4. Be realistic about your accomplishments. It is better to be an outstanding teacher than a terrible doctor, no matter what your mother thinks. (If she complains, tell her you wish she had married a millionaire since it would have made your life a lot easier, but you're willing to live and let live, if she is. (See Ecclesiastes 9:3).

5. If the strain is too great, quit your job. Really. Let's face it, you aren't successful if you are miserable. Don't give yourself headaches and ulcers by compromising your principles. Get into a line of work you can be proud of and in which you are motivated to do well.

6. Keep in mind that some people are prone to jealousy. So, if someone tries to tell you that you don't deserve to be where you are, just consider the source. Maintain your self-confidence. You're on top because you worked for it.

Although the word **success** appears nowhere in the King James version of the New Testament, the apostle John offers a perfect definition of success when he writes to Gaius, "Beloved, I wish above all things that thou mayest prosper and be in health, even as thy soul prospereth" (3 John 2).

What then is success? A prosperous life, good health, and a righteous soul. In short, nothing to be terrified about.

**"Goals should be diverse
and balanced so that
they help you improve
spiritually, financially,
and socially."**

Chapter 18:

Setting Proper Goals

Targets, goals, directions, and priorities are the factors that cut a path to success. Life cannot be ad-libbed. To help your friends and co-workers learn how to set worthy goals, make the following suggestions:

1. Goals should always be God-honoring.
2. Goals should be realistic, yet challenging.
3. Goals must be written down on paper and read twice daily.
4. Goals should be diverse and balanced so that they help you improve spiritually, mentally, physically, financially, and socially.
5. Goals must be supported by specific action plans designed to help you reach the goals.
6. Goals must be reviewed, analyzed, and revised at pre-determined set intervals (weekly, monthly, or quarterly).

"The key to motivating
others will always come
down to this: The more
you can provide people
with what they want, the
more they will respond to
what your wants are.**"**

Chapter 19:

Effective Listening Skills

Before you can motivate other people, you must know what they want. The key to motivating others will always come down to this: The more you can provide people with what they want, the more they will respond to what your wants are.

A six-year-old child may be motivated by the promise of a gold star on his or her Sunday school lesson. A sixteen-year-old may be motivated by an offer to loan him or her the family car on Friday night. A thirty-six-year-old may be motivated by the promise of a job transfer. A sixty-six-year-old may be motivated by the chance to earn extra income.

If you can learn what people want, you can meet your needs by responding to theirs.

But how do you learn what other people's wants are? Simply by listening to them. But listening so that you truly hear what people are saying and so that the speakers know you have heard and understood them. Let's see how that can be accomplished.

Lend Me Your Ears

A great irony of our American educational system is that it emphasizes studying the communication skills we spend the least time using.

Consider this: As infants we began to listen the moment we were born; but, in our school systems we spent absolutely no time studying how to be effective listeners. As babies, we began to speak at about age one; but, most of our school systems offered only one year of training in public speaking.

Conversely, you now spend fewer than two hours per day involved in some form of writing; nevertheless, you spent more than twelve years learning how to write.

With such an inverted educational focus, it isn't difficult to understand why many people are ineffective public speakers and inadequate listeners. Listening, particularly, seems to be a lost talent. As Psalm 115:6 notes, "They have ears, but they hear not."

People today are flocking to professional counselors (and paying them top dollar) because they so desperately want someone to listen to them. Televisions don't listen. Radios, VCRs, record players, and cassette tape players don't listen. We live in an era of noise, and hurting individuals are pleading for someone to listen to them over the din of the world's cacophonous blast.

We Christians have heard the comforting words of a "still small voice." It has given us the answer to life's problems. Now, we must develop a ministry of listening so that we can hear the needs of those who are yet lost. Through sensitive discernment, we will know how to properly minister to those who come to us with personal and spiritual needs. We can also motivate them to reach their full potential as individuals.

Let's review some basic ways in which you can become a better listener. In so doing, we will also improve your relationships with people you have opportunities to witness to, minister to, and motivate.

First, remember to **maintain eye contact** with the person speaking to you. If your eyes are focused on the other person's eyes (instead of staring off into space or glancing at a newspaper in your hands), the speaker will know that he or she has your undivided attention. This will give the person a feeling that you are taking seriously what is being said.

Second, use **good body language.** Use postures that emphasize you are paying attention. Sit near the other person, not across the room. Lean slightly forward, as though you truly desire to hear every word being spoken. Occasionally nod your head affirmatively as to announce without words your agreement with or understanding of what is being said.

Third, listen closely to what is being said and **keep your mind on**

the topic at hand. Don't let your mind wander. Don't try to anticipate what the other person is going to say next, and don't spend a
lot of time trying to make up clever responses. If you are really
paying attention, you'll grasp the complete intent of what the
other person is saying. In doing this, your responses will later
come very naturally. In most instances, once you know the complete circumstances of a given need or situation, there will probably
be only one or two practical solutions. These solutions will become
obvious to you as you hear your person's full story.

Fourth, **use short lulls in conversation** and moments of silence
to add weight to your discussions. Selling bottle openers or magazines door to door may call for a fast-talking person; but, personal
credibility and individual trust are earned only when people believe
you have taken the time to think carefully about what you are
going to say before you open your mouth. By taking a moment
before responding to your friend's conversation, you will give the
impression that your mind has been completely occupied with
what he or she has been saying; now, you are taking a moment to
reflect on it and to formulate a proper response. This substantiates
your reputation as a good listener.

Fifth, remember to **observe common courtesy.** Don't cut someone off in the middle of a sentence and don't stifle conversations
by injecting negative remarks. Don't talk along with people, echo-
ing their words and anticipating them; if you have this nervous
habit, start controlling it. Don't put words into people's mouths; let
them explain things their own way. Don't expend energy by lying
in wait to jump on whoever is talking the moment that person
says something you don't agree with.

And to your five rules for effective listening, you should also
remember to add a point about using positive responses. Once you
have convinced someone that you are a caring listener, you won't
want to do anything that might damage your relationship. So,
when you do speak, make references to what you heard the other
person say. And always begin with positive statements, even when
you need to disagree with something. Say, "You sure hit home on
a real problem there, but my concern about what you said is
that. . . ."

The key is to show through your appearance, your behavior,

and your eventual responses that you have given your complete attention to what the other person has had to say.

Good listeners are few in number. Many people don't realize the importance of being a sensitive and caring listener; nor do they know how to improve their listening skills. You are no longer in that category. You've learned the five rules for improving listening skills. Now, let's see what you do with this earful of information.

Chapter 20:

Ten Ways to Show You Value Others

G reet people by name, proving you really know who they are.

- Make a point to learn something about the other family members of your employees, colleagues, and partners.
- Visit people where they work if it poses no problem. Learn about the work they do.
- Meet one-on-one with people and ask their opinions and advice on several matters.
- Whenever you make an error, say to the other person, "I made a mistake and I'm sorry" or "You were right and I've learned something from this."
- If you must criticize, do it orally; if you want to praise, send it in a letter or card (that the recipient can show to others).
- When one person complains to you about someone else, respond with, "How can we work together to help this person?"
- When differences of opinion create arguments or debates, focus on the issues of the matter rather than the personalities of the people involved.
- Create a sharing environment wherein employees or friends can feel safe in communicating anything to you without fear of reprisal.
- Smile, and give people the benefit of the doubt rather than automatically thinking the worst of them.

"Seest thou a man diligent in his business? he shall stand before kings; he shall not stand before mean men."

—Proverbs 22:29

Chapter 21:

Pushing the Right Buttons

H aving once heard the needs of other people, you then need to use this knowledge to help motivate these people. Always remember that people are motivated by what the end-all benefits will be to them. For example, people do not buy books, they buy information. They do not buy potatoes, they buy good taste and nourishment. They do not attend churches, they attend congregations where fellowship, love, and ministry are provided.

To motivate people, you must know what benefits will stimulate them as well as know how to convince them that you can help them obtain those benefits. In tandem with this, you will be directing them along a path of action that can make their work beneficial to others, too. For example, if you can motivate one of your church's Sunday school teachers to take a course in public speaking because it will help her or him at the job, you also will be enhancing this teacher's ability to teach Sunday school more effectively. The person's personal gain will have spin-off value for others.

To make a machine work properly, you must know which buttons to push to operate it. To motivate people to achieve something, you must know which symbolic buttons to push. Basically, there are three buttons that work: **threats, incentives,** and **inducement.**

For a variety of reasons, the use of threats is the least-preferred method of motivation: it seems to negate the Christian tenets of love and charity; it must be constantly enforced; its results are not as long lasting or perpetual; and it requires unpleasant direct confrontation. Nevertheless, there are instances in which threats are justified. Life needs to have its balances, and the threat of retaliation or recompense can provide such balances. The Law of Moses in the Old Testament was direct in explaining the punishments that would be meted out if certain offenses were committed. Today, our modern laws related to accepted civil conduct are enforced by the threat of fines, imprisonment, or death for those who violate them. Admittedly, these are extreme measures, but they are necessary for handling extreme circumstances.

As Christians, our role is not to browbeat or scare or force people into doing our bidding. It is not wrong, however, for us to motivate someone to do right by reminding him or her about the dangerous consequences of his or her actions (Galatians 6:1). As parents, we must use appropriate measures of correction with our children (Proverbs 23:13); as workers, we must accept rules and standards set forth by our employers (Ephesians 6:5); and, as church leaders, we must be disciplined by the high calling of our office (1 Timothy 3:2-8). Indeed, threats and warnings are true motivators, but they are as dangerous for the user as they are for the person being threatened. Proceed with great caution whenever you decide to use this form of motivation.

The second great motivator is the use of incentives. We all respond to incentives. Your weekly salary is an incentive for you to go to work each day. A trip to Hawaii is an incentive for you to try to win this year's sales contest. A medal is an incentive for maintaining a perfect military record. The blue ribbon is an incentive for grooming and training your cat or dog for the pet show.

Knowing that incentives work, however, is not the same as knowing how they work. Incentives only work as motivators when they are matched with the people who desire them. For example, a well-known corporation conducted a five-year study to discover what its most successful incentives had been for employees. Surprisingly, the results of the study showed that no particular incentive was any more successful overall than another. A closer analysis revealed that each incentive had appealed to a different group of people. An offer of more money had been successful in motivating people who wanted or needed more money; an offer of more authority or a more prestigious job title had been successful in motivating people who had money but now wanted more power; an offer of extra fringe benefits had been successful in motivating senior executives who already had good salaries and prestigious titles but wanted more "perks," such as extra vacation time and a private parking space.

The lesson found in that five-year study was that people are motivated by different incentives, and people will change their incentives as they go through different phases of their lives and careers. As a leader, you will need to monitor the needs and desires of the people you manage or work with so that the incentives you offer them will remain pertinent to the times and phases of their lives.

Scientists who study human behavior, such as Abraham Maslow, B. F. Skinner, and Carl Jung have determined that human beings have a "hierarchy of needs" that helps to determine which incentives will motivate them at different times of their lives or under varied circumstances. In his book *Motivation and Personality*, Maslow sets the priorities of human needs this way:

1. Physical Needs (air, water, food)
2. Safety Needs (clothing, shelter, defenses)
3. Love Needs (affection, sense of belonging)
4. Esteem Needs (strength, fame, glory, competence)
5. Self-Actualization Needs (talent mastery, fulfilled destiny)

As Christians, we recognize these innate tendencies within our being, but we also strive to rise above self-centered glorification. Christ has taught us to love our enemies, to befriend the needy, to teach the gospel, to protect the weak, and to behave humbly. Our base nature is to be selfish, greedy, ambitious, proud, and independent. Conversely, our spiritual nature is to be forgiving, helpful, concerned, friendly, and meek. Here, then, is a war.

How can a Christian properly use incentives as a motivation tool without simultaneously encouraging the base side of human nature to become a dominating factor? There are three answers to this question:

1. By establishing standards. A high level of excellence should be set for every job or goal. If the job is performed according to the set standards, the worker and his or her employer can both feel satisfied. If the worker surpasses even these very high standards, however, then a greater reward is justified. But rewards and incentives should not be necessary in order to motivate workers to strive for excellence anyway.

2. By selecting incentives that are God-honoring. Too many companies are offering shameful incentives to their workers or clients these days. Sinful incentives include alcoholic beverages, pornographic movies, illegal kick backs, bribes, illicit sex, narcotics, and access to company cars or properties for personal use. Christ has admonished us to lay up treasures in heaven and not to be seduced by worldly wooings.

3. By selecting incentives that are personal and functional. Sports teams do not like to win games by default. There is no challenge or honor in this. Similarly, people should not be "honored" for showing up for work. They should be honored for the kind of work they do. And when honored, they should be presented a personal award. Rather than a ten-year pin (like everyone else), they could be given something that reflects their enjoyments: dinner at a nice restaurant; a sewing machine; a good book; a camera; a reference Bible; a briefcase; an out-door grill; a radio; a rod and reel; or a set of tools.

There is nothing wrong with trying to motivate people by offering incentives. The key thing is to evaluate the type of incentive and the reason for offering it.

The third great motivator is inducement. By offering them a new way of life, Christ persuaded twelve men to become his disciples. By convincing him that he had a great mission before him, Paul persuaded Timothy to read and study the Scriptures diligently.

Whenever we use logic, emotions, imagination, or influence to persuade people to think the way we think, we have induced them to be on our side. This also motivates them to serve the same aims and ideals we serve. As long as these are Christ-honoring and noble, they are worthy actions.

The key to successful persuasion is to make things positive. The way to sell diet plans is not to warn about heart disease and cholesterol build-up but, instead, to promise a slender figure and an attractive appearance. The way to convince children to avoid alcohol is not to read them statistics about liver ailments or teenage auto accidents, but to remind them of how much you admire them for not yielding to the coaxings and teasings of their peers who are less disciplined. The best sort of inducement motivation is the act of encouraging people to be the very best they can be at all they do. It may take regular calls or notes or talks or pats on the backs, but as long as it remains a positive force it will also remain a motivating force.

Summary

In this part we learned that the motivational skills you mastered for your personal betterment in Parts 1, 2, and 3 could find companion outlets in also motivating other people. We discovered that people must first be taught how to want success enough not to flee from it once they are about to achieve it. We also discovered that in order for you to know how to motivate the people with whom you work and associate, you must learn how to listen carefully to their needs, dreams, concerns, and desires.

Having learned ways to know about people's wants, we then learned how to use these wants to motivate them by using threats, incentives, and inducements. Over and again we were cautioned never to try any form of motivation unless it serves the person being motivated and honors God.

Be motivated now to do something significant with your life.

"Seest thou a man diligent in his business? he shall stand before kings; he shall not stand before mean men" (Proverbs 22:29).

Helping Others Set Goal Priorities

One of the best ways to help other people reach their goals is to show them the importance of doing the most crucial things first. In order to determine priorities, ask the person you are trying to encourage to answer the following questions:

1. What weight should I be at?
2. In what ways could my physical condition be improved?
3. When do I want to buy my next car? next home?
4. How much retirement income do I want to have saved by age sixty-five?
5. Where and when do I want my next vacation to be?
6. What social and civic activities would I enjoy joining?
7. When can I reduce my current debt load?
8. What sorts of business honors do I desire?
9. When will I begin to spend more time with my family?
10. What additional education do I need to obtain?
11. Which clients and prospects do I want to serve more professionally?
12. How can I serve my church in a more direct way?
13. When can I begin a new Bible study program?
14. How can I become a more effective witness to non-Christians?
15. How can I show support for the pastor and other leaders in my church?
16. When would I like to expand my business?
17. How much money do I want to earn this year?
18. Which old friendships would I like to rekindle?
19. When do I plan to review my total insurance coverage?
20. In what ways can I improve my wardrobe?
21. When will I have my will drawn up (or updated)?
22. How disciplined is my moral and religious life?
23. Which five books should I try to read very soon?
24. My greatest yet-unfulfilled life's ambition is what?
25. How can I find more time for prayer and meditation?

Suggested Readings on Motivation

Asbell, Bernard and Clair F. Vough. *Tapping the Human Resource: A Strategy for Productivity.* New York: Amacom, 1975.

Black, Kenneth and G. Hugh Russell. *Human Behavior in Business.* Englewood Cliffs: Prentice-Hall, 1972.

Demaray, Donald E. *Laughter, Joy and Healing.* Grand Rapids: Baker Book House, 1986.

Dudley, Donald and Elton Welke. *How to Survive Being Alive.* New York: Signet Books, 1977.

Eilon, Samuel. *Management Control.* London: MacMillan & Co., 1971.

Foster, Richard J. *Celebration of Discipline: Paths to Spiritual Growth.* New York: Harper & Row, 1978.

Gilbert, Thomas F. *Human Competence: Engineering Worthy Performance.* New York: McGraw-Hill Book Co., 1978.

Hensley, Dennis E. *How to Manage Your Time: Time Management Strategies for Active Christians.* Anderson, Ind.: Warner Press, 1988.

Kahn, Elayne and David A. Rudnitsky. *1001 Ways You Reveal Your Personality.* New York: Signet Books, 1982.

Maltz, Maxwell. *Psycho-Cybernetics.* Englewood Cliffs: Prentice Hall, 1960.

Maslow, Abraham H. *Motivation and Personality.* New York: Harper & Row, 1970.

McGregor, Douglas. *The Human Side of Enterprise.* New York: McGraw-Hill Book Co., 1960.

Pietsch, William T. *Human Be-ing: How to Have a Creative Relationship Instead of a Power Struggle.* New York: Signet Books, 1975.

Rainey, Dennis and Barbara. *Building Your Mate's Self-Esteem.* San Bernardino: Here's Life Publishers, 1986.

Roseman, Edward. *Confronting Nonpromotability: How to Manage a Stalled Career.* New York: Amacom, 1977.

Schoenberg, Robert J. *The Art of Being a Boss.* New York: Mentor Executive Library, 1978.

Tec, Leon. *Targets: How to Set Goals for Yourself & Reach Them.* New York: Signet Books, 1980.